10/13

Writing Builders
Will and Wendy Build a
WEBSITE
WITH
DIGITAL TOOLS

by Darice Bailer
illustrated by Sean O'Neill

Content Consultant
Jan Lacina, Ph.D.
College of Education
Texas Christian University

NORWOODHOUSE PRESS
CHICAGO, ILLINOIS

Dedication: The author would like to thank Deborah Goldstein, Library/
Media Specialist at Purchase School in Harrison, New York, and the
students in Tiffany Vaccari's second-grade class at Old Greenwich School in
Connecticut for helping her with this book!

Norwood House Press
P.O. Box 316598
Chicago, Illinois 60631
For information regarding Norwood House Press, please visit
our website at:
www.norwoodhousepress.com or call 866-565-2900.

Editor: Melissa York
Designer: Craig Hinton
Project Management: Red Line Editorial

Library of Congress Cataloging-in-Publication Data
Bailer, Darice.
  Will and Wendy build a website / by Darice Bailer ; illustrated by Sean
O'Neill.
      pages cm. -- (Writing builders)
  Summary: "Will and Wendy create a website when Will moves to
Australia. They learn how to add pictures, create new web pages, and
add stories to their website allowing them to share information. Concepts
include: writing, revising, and publishing. Activities in the back help the
reader create their own website"--Provided by publisher.
  Includes bibliographical references and index.
  ISBN 978-1-59953-584-5 (library edition : alkaline paper)
  ISBN 978-1-60357-564-5 (ebook)
1. Web sites--Design--Juvenile literature. 2. Authorship--Juvenile
literature. 3. Editing--Juvenile literature. 4. Web publishing--Juvenile
literature. I. O'Neill, Sean, 1968- illustrator. II. Title.
  TK5105.888.B346 2013
  006.7--dc23
                                      2013010589

Words in **black bold** are defined in the glossary.

Our Class Website

This year, my best friend Will and I built a website. We thought only grown-ups could set up websites, but it turns out kids can too! Our website is a group of pages about our class, 3G. Our teacher, Mrs. Gold, helped us get started. We learned that if we can write and type on the computer, we can publish a website!

Will isn't in Mrs. Gold's class anymore. He moved to a new country that is nearly 10,000 miles away from school. Can you guess which country it is? It's the smallest continent and the largest island in the world! Luckily, Will just has to type in our website address to see what is going on with our class.

Will and I discovered that creating a website is as easy as writing a story. You come up with an idea and think about what should be on the website. You organize your ideas on separate web pages and use your best words. Now Will can stay in touch with us from far away.

By Wendy, Class 3G Web Designer, age 9

Wendy didn't know what was wrong with Will. They were supposed to be working on their research reports during computer lab time, but Will had stopped typing. He mumbled, "I don't want to move."

"Move where?" asked Wendy.

"To Australia," Will groaned. "My dad has a new job. I have to leave Mrs. Gold's class and make all new friends."

"Oh no," said Wendy. "I'm so sorry you're leaving!"

Wendy stared at the website on Will's computer. Suddenly, she had a wonderful idea. "Will, we can make a class website!"

Will looked up. What was Wendy talking about? He thought creating a website was too hard for nine-year-olds.

"We can set it up together!" Wendy said excitedly. "Mrs. Gold will help during computer lab time. Then when you're gone, the class can write our news on the website. You can read all about us online."

Mrs. Gold came over and Wendy shared her idea. "What a great way to practice writing and stay in touch!" said Mrs. Gold. "Good writing is as important on a website as in a story or journal."

"Our classroom website can be a place to read the latest class news," continued Mrs. Gold. "Will and his new class can read reviews of our favorite books. And there can be more than that! Our website can show photos of our class. We can even upload videos!"

Mrs. Gold leaned over and typed in the school's website address in the white **browser** box: www.winwardschool.org. The school's red and blue home page appeared. It said, "Welcome to Winward School!"

"Did you know a website is the home of a group of pages on the Internet?" asked Mrs. Gold. "All those linked pages are called the World Wide Web."

"So that's why it's called a website," said Will.

Mrs. Gold said, "A website is like a story that never ends. We can **post** new text and photos every day."

"So how do we start making our website?" Wendy asked.

Mrs. Gold smiled. "Excellent question! We're going to need a **domain** name. A domain name is the website address. It's what you type to bring up the site."

"Like www.winwardschool.org?" Will asked.

Mrs. Gold said, "Exactly."

"How do you get a domain name?" Will asked.

"Our class can set up a website using our school's system," said Mrs. Gold. "If you make a website on your own, there are many companies that host websites. A host company has a powerful computer, called a **server**, that stores countless websites."

"Can we start?" asked Wendy.

"I'll set up a class website in our school's system this afternoon," promised Mrs. Gold.

Class 3G had computer lab time the next afternoon. "We're all set!" Mrs. Gold said as she sat down with Wendy and Will at a computer. "Our class website will be www.winwardschool.org/class3g."

"What does the slash mean?" asked Wendy.

"The text after the slash, 'class3g,' is the name of the web page within the larger website, www.winwardschool.org. It will take Will or anybody else straight to our class's page."

Will opened the web editing program on the computer. Will and Wendy saw a toolbar. It had all the tools Will and Wendy needed to design their website. They could start a new website, add pages to their website, save and upload their work, or change the way their website looked.

Document 1

Title

Head

Text

Text

Format

Font:

Verdana

Style: **Size:**

Regular   12

Color: TT   Tᴛ   T   Ŧ

Link: **Image:**

Cancel   OK

Link

Link

Link

Link

Will clicked "new" to start a new website. The program asked them to choose a **template**, or design.

"A template makes it easy to start building a website," Mrs. Gold explained. "You just type in your own title and text, or words. When we're done, the program will upload the web page to the Internet."

Wendy looked up at Mrs. Gold. "So we can just pick a design and get started?"

Mrs. Gold nodded. "How easy is that?"

"Cool!" Will said. The children saw a design they both liked. It had a blue background and a picture of a brown dog.

"But the template has words on it," Wendy said disappointedly.

"And we can change them!" Mrs. Gold said. "Move your cursor over to the title on the template."

Will did. *Click.* "A box!" Will said. "There's a box around the title!"

"Right," Mrs. Gold said. "That means you can edit the title now. Click on it and hit the delete key." Wendy did, and one by one the letters disappeared.

Will looked up at Mrs. Gold. "What should we type now?"

"A title for our website," Mrs. Gold said.

"I've got it!" cried Wendy. "Welcome to Mrs. Gold's Class."

Mrs. Gold smiled. "Sounds good to me!"

In another text box, Will typed a few more sentences.

Hello! Welcome to Class 3G! We're in third grade in Mrs. Gold's class at Winward School. Our favorite things are gym and recess. We're trying to be good writers.

Their home page was ready! They clicked "upload" on the toolbar. Next, Mrs. Gold helped the kids set up more pages for their website. She created two new pages titled "News" and "Stories." The names of the two pages showed up in a column on the left-hand side of the home page.

Will and Wendy were ready to post news on the website. "Remember what Mrs. Gold told us," Wendy reminded Will. "We shouldn't write things on the Internet that aren't safe for a stranger to read."

"No addresses or full names either," agreed Will. "And Mrs. Gold or another adult should read what we write before we post it."

Will pressed the middle of his glasses up on his nose and started thinking. He had a great idea! He gave his story a headline, a byline, and a dateline, just like a real reporter. These tell readers the title, author, date, and location of the story.

Pajama Day
by Will
Winward, Connecticut,
November 10—Yesterday was
Pajama Day at school. I wore
my pajamas. So did everyone.
We wore our pajamas all day
long. Then we went home.

Mrs. Gold peered over Will's shoulder. "Great start! But don't forget to color it in with details. Writers are like painters, only they paint with words. What did you feel? Use your senses and words that describe your feelings.

Will thought some more, then kept typing.

Yesterday was Pajama Day at Winward School. Everyone wore pajamas, even the grown-ups. One of the third-grade teachers, Mrs. Gold, had little pink cupcakes on her blue pajama bottoms. I wore a long pair of soft red pajamas with blue whales on them and blue feet. It felt weird wearing pajamas on the bus to school.

I hope my new school in Australia knows about Pajama Day. It's fun!

Mrs. Gold smiled. "Much better!"

But Will frowned and shook his head. "I wish I could draw a picture like I do with stories on paper," he said. "To make them more interesting."

"Well," said Mrs. Gold, "a parent took some photos of us on Pajama Day. The photos are up on the school website. Let's add a **hyperlink** to that site."

"What's a hyperlink?" asked Will.

"A hyperlink takes readers from one page to another on the Internet, such as between our class website and the Pajama Day photos. A hyperlink can look like one word, several words, or even an image. It also has directions for the web browser. The reader can't see the directions, but when we write the website, we have to include them."

Mrs. Gold helped Will find the button on the toolbar to insert a hyperlink. A box popped up. Will typed in what he wanted the hyperlink to say: "Photos." He also had to type in the directions, or the website address where the hyperlink would lead.

Bingo. Now the photos were just one click away!

File   Edit   Page   Style   Connect   View   Help

Welcome to Mrs. Gold's Class

Welcome to

Home
News
Stories

Welcome to

Pajama Day

by Will

Winward

10—Yester

School. Eve

the grown-ups. One of the third g

teachers, Mrs. Gold, had little pink

cupcakes on her blue pajama bott

I wore a long pair of soft red paja

with blue whales on them and blu

feet. It felt weird wearing pajama

Hyperlink

Hyperlink Text:

Photos

Hyperlink Address:

www.

Meanwhile, Wendy was hard at work on her own story.

Pet Photo Contest
by Wendy
Winward, Connecticut, November 10—
One day, our teachers offered prizes. They were prizes for the best photos. You could win a gift certificate to the school book fair.

Mrs. Gold looked at Wendy's screen.

"Wendy, you want to explain to your readers why the school asked students to bring in pictures. What did they show? Make sure your writing is clear so your readers aren't confused."

Wendy sighed. Whether she was writing a story at her desk or at the computer, she always had to edit her work! But she knew good organization would help people understand her writing.

Welcome to Mrs.

Pet Photo Contest

by Wendy

Winward, Connecticut, November 10—Last week, Winward School had a Pet Photo Contest. Our principal said we could bring in photos of our pets. Then she and the teachers would look at all the photos and give out prizes. The prize was a gift certificate to the school book fair.

The Funniest award went to a golden retriever. That big yellow dog stood on its back legs wearing a green skirt. The Sportiest was a tiny white mouse driving a red sports car. Patrick's fat white cat won the Cleverest award. She was listening to music on an iPod! Next year, I hope I can teach my dog Sadie to do some funny tricks.

Mrs. Gold brought her camera to school the next day. Everyone lined up against the bulletin board so she could take a class photo. Then she took a photo of each student. Finally, the only person left was Mrs. Gold! *Snap*! Will took a picture of her.

"For the website!" Mrs. Gold said.

Will and Wendy watched as Mrs. Gold put the photos on the website. First, she downloaded the photos from the camera into a folder on the computer. She opened the web editing program and clicked on the template where she wanted each photo to go. She followed the steps in the program to choose the photos from her folder, and then she clicked "upload."

"Nice," smiled Wendy.

There was a big going-away party for Will the following week. Mrs. Gold brought in ice cream with pastel rainbow sprinkles and marshmallow topping. And Mrs. Gold gave Will a card with the class photo. Inside, the class had signed their names.

When Will arrived in Australia, he couldn't wait to get on the Internet and see the class website. Mrs. Gold was right. Even though it was really thousands of miles from Australia and 20 hours by plane, his old school was just a few clicks away.

Will typed the website address in his browser, www.winwardschool.org/class3g. Before he could lean back in his chair, he was smiling. He could see his class, his teacher—his friends. There they were on the home page, with the hyperlinks for the other pages with news and stories.

The website also had a new page called "For Will." When Will clicked on the hyperlink, he saw photos of all his friends. The caption under Wendy's photo said, "I miss my writing buddy!"

Under "News," Will found a story that Wendy wrote about him. The page also had a hyperlink to a website with facts about Australia.

http://www.winwardschool.org/class3g

e to Mrs. Gold's Class

Welcome to Mrs

Class 3G Loses a Friend

by Wendy

Winward, Connecticut, November 28 — Thanksgiving, one of the students in Clas very far away. Will moved to Australia w father took a new job there.

Luckily, the Class 3G teacher, Mrs. Gold her students how to build a website. Here website, Will can see photos of his friends read all the class news.

Class 3G is learning a lot about Australia. say Australians live down under because th on a continent below the equator. Australia themselves Aussies. Class 3G also learned t is probably wearing shorts while we are wea mittens! That's because when it's summer i Australia, it's winter in the Northern Hemisp

Class 3G Loses a Friend
by Wendy

Winward, Connecticut, November 28 — Over Thanksgiving, one of the students in Class 3G moved very far away. Will moved to Australia when his father took a new job there.

Luckily, the Class 3G teacher, Mrs. Gold, taught her students how to build a website. Here on the website, Will can see photos of his friends and read all the class news.

Class 3G is learning a lot about Australia. People say Australians live down under because they live on a continent below the equator. Australians call themselves Aussies. Class 3G also learned that Will is probably wearing shorts while we are wearing mittens! That's because when it's summer in Australia, it's winter in the Northern Hemisphere.

Will smiled when he read Wendy's post. He knew she had edited her writing and written as clearly as she could.

Will felt happier as he closed the website for dinner. The next day, he would show the website to his new class. He couldn't wait to teach his new friends all about websites.

You Can Build a Website, Too!

It's easy to get started on your own website. All you need is an idea, a plan, a little setup, and some good writing!

First, ask yourself some questions:
1. What is the purpose of the website I want to build? Maybe it's to share information with other people. For example, maybe you want to post photos from your birthday party or summer vacation so your grandparents can see them.

2. What will I call my website? When you come up with a name, check to see if someone already owns it. You can type www.-----.com in your browser, or check your host website.

3. Who will look at my website? Keep in mind who will read your website. If you're creating a website for your classmates, make sure it's something they would be interested in.

Now, get started!
1. Sign Up! Ask a parent or teacher to help you sign up for a domain name. Then you can choose a template and get started!

2. Set Up! Type in the names of your pages, one at a time.

3. Write! The same rules for good writing still hold! Begin sentences with capital letters. Write clearly. Use the best descriptive words you can.

4. Edit and Revise! Read your story aloud to make sure it flows smoothly. Correct your spelling. Ask a friend or two to read what you've written. Ask them what they like about your website and also what they would change.

5. Publish! Before you press the publish key on your website, let an adult double-check what you've written. You don't want to give out too much private information to strangers around the world. It's not safe to include last names, addresses, or telephone numbers that everyone can see. Some templates help you keep your website private. Then only people who know your password can log on and see what you wrote.

6. Be Class Writing Buddies with Another School. You could start a fiction story, post it, and let the other class finish! They can e-mail your teacher their story ending. What fun!

Glossary

browser: a computer program that helps you find information on the Internet and arrive at a website.

domain: a location on the Internet.

hyperlink: a connection, or link, between one spot on a website and another, or a link between one website and another.

post: to enter new writing on the web page, or the writing itself.

server: a powerful computer that can hold a lot of information and run many programs.

template: a design or guide you can use to create your website.

For More Information

Books

Cornwall, Phyllis. *Online Etiquette and Safety*. Ann Arbor, MI: Cherry Lake Publishing, 2010.

Herrington, Lisa M. *Internet Safety*. New York: Children's Press, 2013.

Websites

Net Smartz Kids
http://www.netsmartzkids.org/
This website has games that teach about Internet safety.

Kids Website Creator
http://kidswebsitecreator.com/#/build-a-site/4541418477
Here's an easy place to create your own website.

About the Author

Darice Bailer loves writing for kids and visiting schools where she can talk to young students about being good writers.